Library of Congress Cataloging-in-Publication Data

Watts, Barrie.
    Honeybee / Barrie Watts.
      p.   cm.—(Stopwatch)
    "First published by A & C Black…Adapted and published in the
United States in 1989 by Silver Burdett Press"—T.p. verso.
    Summary: Describes the life cycle and behavior of the honeybee.
    1. Honeybee—Juvenile literature. [1. Honeybee. 2. Bees.]
I. Title. II. Series: Stopwatch books.
QL568.A6W375   1989
595.79′9—dc20   89-38981
  ISBN 0-382-24013-8   CIP
  ISBN 0-382-24011-1 (lib. bdg.)   AC

First published by A & C Black (Publishers) Limited
35 Bedford Row, London WC1R 4JH

© 1989 Barrie Watts

Adapted and published in the United States in 1990
by Silver Burdett Press, Englewood Cliffs, New Jersey
U.S. project editor: Nancy Furstinger

Acknowledgments
The illustrations are by Helen Senior.

The author and publisher would like to thank Michael Chinery, and
David Blackwood, beekeeper, for his help and advice without which
many of the photographs in this book could not have been taken.

Printed in Belgium by Proost International Book Production

Honeybee

Barrie Watts

Silver Burdett Press • Englewood Cliffs, New Jersey

Here is a bee.

Do you like to eat honey?

Honey is made by bees. The bee in the photograph is collecting nectar from a flower. Nectar is a sweet juice hidden inside the flower. Bees make the nectar into honey.

This book will tell you about the life of a bee.

Bees live in a hive.

Bees make honey in a hive, like this one.

As many as fifty thousand bees live in one beehive.
People keep beehives in gardens and orchards.

Inside the hive, bees live on a honeycomb. The big
photograph shows the honeycomb up close.

The bees make the honeycomb out of wax. The wax
comes from their bodies. Each hole in the honeycomb
has six wax walls. These holes are called cells.

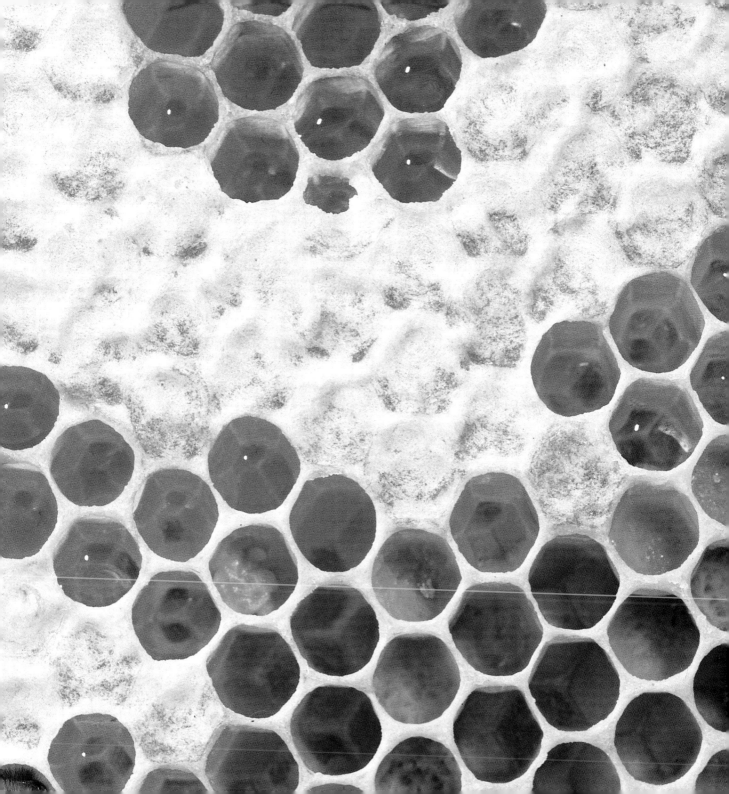

Worker bees look after the hive.

Look at the photograph. The bees on this honeycomb are called worker bees. They protect the hive. These worker bees are storing honey in the honeycomb. When the cells are full, the bees cover them with wax.

There are three kinds of bees in a beehive.

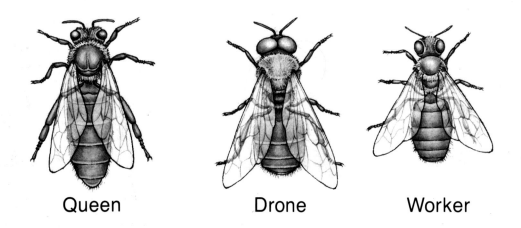

Queen   Drone   Worker

There is one big queen bee. There are hundreds of male bees called drones. There are thousands of smaller worker bees. Worker bees are female but they cannot lay eggs.

The queen bee lays her eggs.

There are always some worker bees with the queen. They feed her and keep her clean. Look at the photograph.

The queen bee is in the middle. The worker bees are stroking and licking her.

Usually the queen bee stays in the hive. She leaves it to mate, then flies back to lay all her eggs.

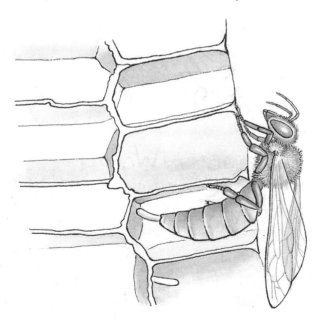

Look at the drawing. The queen bee has started to lay her eggs in the hive.

The eggs are tiny.

The queen bee lays her eggs in the middle part of the honeycomb. She lays one egg in each cell.

In summer the queen can lay hundreds of eggs every day. Each egg sticks to the bottom of the cell.

Look at the big photograph. This shows an egg up close. The egg looks very big. In real life, it is no bigger than a pinhead.

The eggs hatch into larvae.

After three days, the eggs hatch. The creatures that come out of the eggs are called larvae. They look like soft white worms.

The larvae live inside the cells. Worker bees feed the larvae with honey and a special food called bee milk.

As the larvae grow bigger, each one fills up its cell. After eight days, the larvae are almost fully grown. Look at the big photograph. Can you see which larvae are the oldest? Which larvae are the youngest?

The larva changes into a pupa.

After nine days, worker bees cover the top of each cell with wax. Inside the cells, each larva begins to change into a pupa.

Look at the big photograph. The side of this cell has been cut away. Inside, the pupa has nearly changed into a bee.

Three weeks after the egg was laid, the bee is fully grown. Now it is ready to come out of the cell.

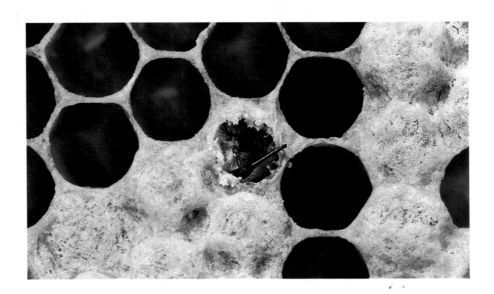

The bee starts to chew its way through the wax.

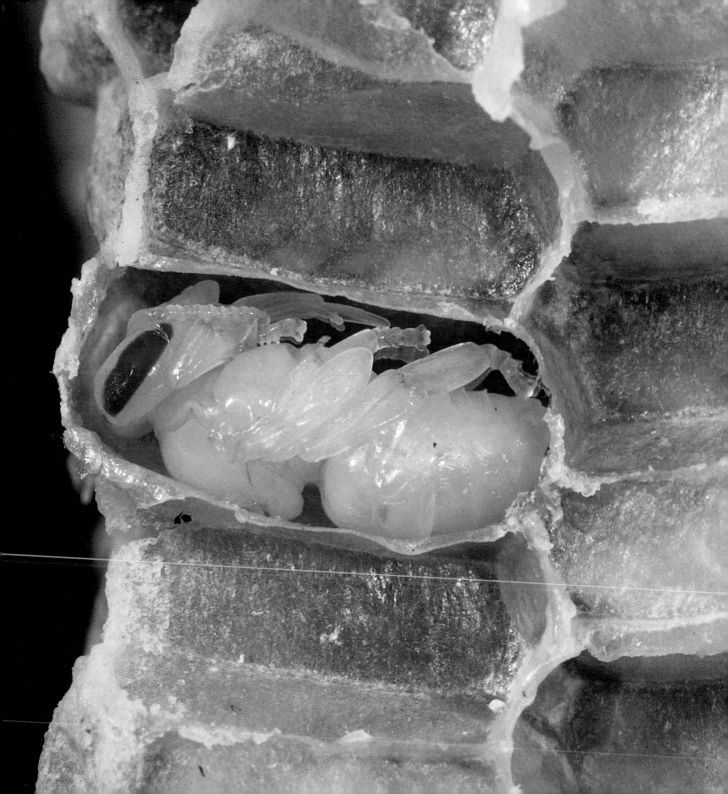

The bee is fully grown.

It takes the bee about an hour to chew its way out of the cell. Sometimes other bees will help it out.

The new bee is soft and pale. It cannot fly yet. For a few days it is fed by the other bees.

After four days, the bee's body is hard. The bee's wings are dry and strong, and it can fly out of the hive.

A queen bee grows in a big cell.

Sometimes there are too many bees in a hive. When this happens, the worker bees build big cells for some of the eggs.

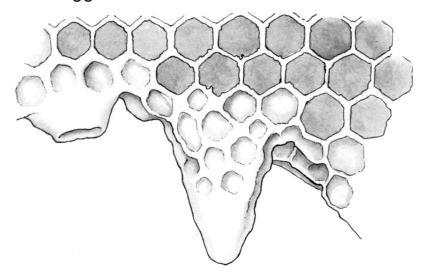

When one of these eggs hatches, the worker bees feed the larva with a special food called royal jelly. This makes the larva grow bigger than the other larvae. It will grow into a new queen bee.

Look at the photograph. The side of this cell has been cut away. You can see the pupa of the queen bee inside.

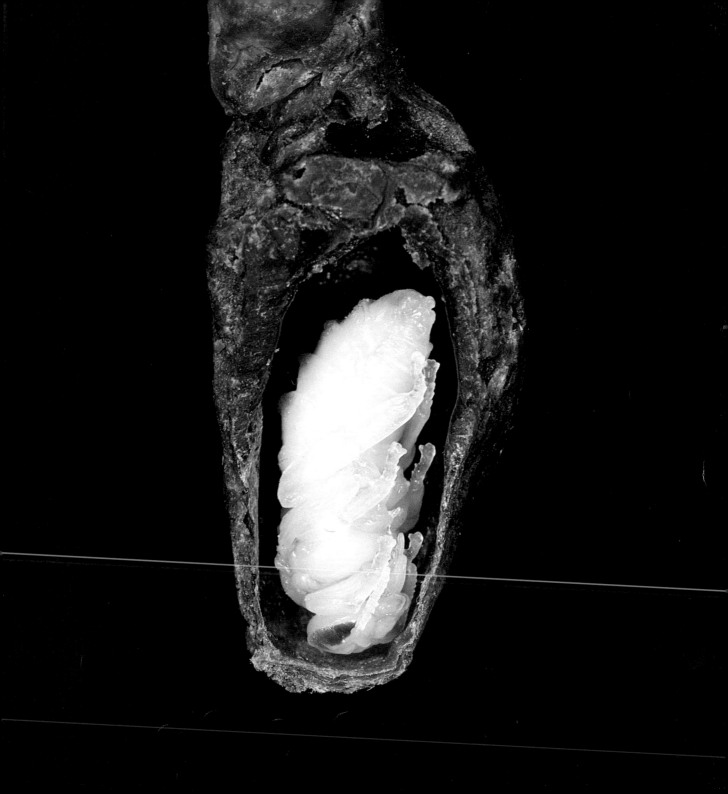

The new queen bee is fully grown.

The new queen bee grows fast. She is fully grown two weeks after hatching from the egg.

Look at the photograph. The queen bee is coming out of her cell. Her body is pale and soft.

Worker bees feed the new queen bee with royal jelly. After a few days, she leaves the hive to mate.

The queen bee is followed by the drones. She will mate with some of the drones. Then the new queen will return to the hive to lay her eggs.

A swarm of bees leaves the hive.

While the new queen is growing in her cell, the old queen bee leaves the hive. She takes some of the worker bees with her to look for a new home. This group of bees is called a swarm.

The swarm in the photograph has settled on a tree. The queen bee is in the middle. She has lots of worker bees around her.

When the bees have found a new home, they start to build a honeycomb. Then the queen bee will lay her eggs.

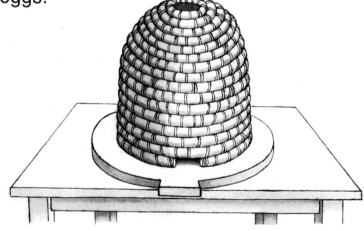

What do you think will happen then?

Do you remember how the bee came from the egg?
See if you can tell the story in your own words.
You can use these pictures to help you.

3

6

Index

This index will help you to find some of the important words in this book.

How many different kinds of honey can you find in the stores?
Look at the different flowers and countries they come from.